HORSE WISDOM

HORSE WISDOM

Life's Lessons from the Saddle

By Melissa Sovey

◢ WILLOW CREEK PRESS

© 2007 Willow Creek Press

Published by Willow Creek Press
P.O. Box 147, Minocqua, Wisconsin 54548

Editor: Andrea Donner
Design: Joy Rasmussen

Photo Credits

© **Christiane Slawik**: pages 2, 5, 8, 15, 16, 23, 24, 27, 28,
31, 32, 35, 40, 43, 47, 51, 55, 56, 60, 63, 64, 68, 75,
80, 84, 88, 91, 92, 95, 96

© **Bob Langrish**: pages 7, 11, 12, 19, 39, 48, 59

© **Linda Shier**: pages 20, 71, 76

© **Edyta Trojanska-Koch**: page 79

© **www.stuewer-tierfoto.de**: pages 36, 44, 52, 67, 72, 83, 87

Printed in Canada

The horse accepts us and can read what's in our hearts;
we must follow his example and trust our own hearts as well…

ACCEPTANCE

*When I'm trusting and being myself
as fully as possible, everything in
my life reflects this by falling into
place easily, often miraculously.*

—Shakti Gawain

Achievement in equitation for both horse and
rider lies in the joy of beautiful, natural movement…

ACHIEVEMENT

*The thing that is really hard, and really amazing,
is giving up on being perfect and beginning
the work of becoming yourself.*

—Anna Quindlen

Riding demands self-awareness, a heightened
understanding of our true nature, and our true desires…

AWARENESS

*To find in ourselves what makes life worth
living is risky business, for it means that
once we know we must seek it.*

—Marsha Sinetar

Simple kindness is one of the truest pleasures, one of the
most sublime and charitable harmonies shared between creatures…

BENEVOLENCE

*The first condition of human
goodness is something to love;
the second, something to revere.*

—George Eliot

Horses strengthen our attributes
and tone our temperaments...

CHARACTER

*No one can leave his character behind
him when he goes on a journey.*

—Yoruba (southern Nigeria) saying

A horse becomes your partner
when he can sense your ease and comfort…

COLLABORATION

*What do we live for, if not to make
life less difficult for each other?*

—George Eliot

Horses have a knack for showing us our strengths when
we are weak, and fortifying our courage when we are fearful…

COMRADERIE

*There is no secret so close as that
between a rider and his horse.*

—R. S. Surtees

There are rides that build trust in yourself,
leaving you ready for the unexpected in the rest of your life.

CONFIDENCE

*The confidence we have in
others stems directly from our
confidence in ourselves.*

—Francois de La Rochefoucauld

Life is an adventure and horses give us
the courage to experience it to the fullest…

COURAGE

*For the most part, fear is nothing
but an illusion. When you share it with
someone else, it tends to disappear.*

—Marilyn C. Barrick

The only thing that
matters is the matter at hand…

DETERMINATION

*In my experience, there is only
one motivation, and that is desire.
No reasons or principles
contain it or stand against it.*

—Jane Smiley

Diligence is a form of loyalty—through the rain, dust storms, blizzards, or baking sun the horse perseveres beneath the saddle…

DILIGENCE

There is no chance, no destiny, no fate, that can circumvent or hinder or control the firm resolve of a determined soul.

—Ella Wheeler Wilcox

Riding, as an art, takes great
discipline, and even greater love…

DISCIPLINE

*There should be no mediocrity
in love, and without love
you cannot create an Art.*

—Nuno Oliveira

Learning to ride is a journey traveled every inch of
the road personally, moment by moment, step by step…

DISCOVERY

*No one can give you Wisdom.
You must discover it for yourself,
on your journey through life,
which no one can take for you.*

—Sun Bear

There is a great satisfaction that comes
when a horse looks to you for direction…

EMPOWERMENT

Knowing is not enough; We must apply.
Willing is not enough; We must do.

—Goethe

When the fantasy and emotion surrounding a horse
settles in the dust, we are still charmed by his presence…

ENCHANTMENT

*The sight of him did something to me
I've never quite been able to explain. He was
more than tremendous strength and speed
and beauty of motion. He set me dreaming.*

—Walt Morley

There is excitement in every inch of the horse. The power and energy waiting to burst forth are contagious...

ENTHUSIASM

In an ordinary mood one would not have been able to accomplish many of the things for which enthusiasm lends one everything, energy, fire.

—Clara Schumann

Horses heighten our sense
of pride, our desire to excel…

EXCELLENCE

*Strive to make something
of yourself; then strive
to make the most of yourself.*

—Alexander Crummel

Clear direction, meaningful actions, mindful intent—
all give horse and rider a steady, unified purpose…

FOCUS

*Obstacles are those frightful
things you see when you
take your eyes off the goal.*

—Hannah More

For some, riding may be the only time
when the burdened soul gets a respite…

FREEDOM

Freedom comes in individual packages.

—Shirley Boone

A horse understands a giving,
caring spirit and responds in kind…

GENEROSITY

Is there a place on him for you to sit
Where your saddle and his soul just fit?

— From *Have You Got The Makings*,
a poem by Bill Dorrance

Equitation is the mindful task of restoring the natural gracefulness of a horse who is now encumbered by a rider...

GRACE

What delights us in visible beauty is the invisible.

—Marie von Ebner-Eschenbach

There is no landscape so
coalesced as one including horses…

HARMONY

Everything in this world which
seems to lack harmony is in reality
the limitation of man's own vision. The
wider the horizon of his observation becomes,
the more harmony of life he enjoys.

—Hazrat Inayat Khan

Working with horses humbles us, makes us aware
that we are not preeminent in the scheme of existence…

HUMILITY

*The only wisdom we can hope
to acquire is the wisdom of
humility. Humility is endless.*

— T.S. Eliot

Suspend all thought for a moment;
depend instead on your intuitive faculties…

INTUITION

Intuition is a spiritual faculty
and does not explain,
but simply points the way.

—Florence Scovel Shinn

Even the heaviest of beasts
carries lightness in his heart...

JOYFULNESS

The joy of a spirit is the
measure of its power.

—Ninon de Lenclos

A horse will first and foremost challenge you to be his leader;
you must challenge yourself to become the best leader possible...

LEADERSHIP

'Submission' is the aim of the dictator.
'Willing participation' is the aspiration of the
thoughtful leader... the true horseman.

—Erik Herbermann

A herd is a family where each member plays
a role and is uniquely bonded to each other...

LOYALTY

We cannot destroy kindred: our
chains stretch a little sometimes,
but they never break.

—Marie de Rabutin-Chantal

It is often the horse who drills, disciplines and develops us
into someone nobler, while we imagine we are his taskmaster…

NOBILITY

*His neigh is like the bidding of a monarch,
and his countenance enforces homage.*

—William Shakespeare

The passion for horses is inexplicable, an ever
present yearning for their company akin to an addiction…

PASSION

*The fiery moments of passionate
experience are the moments of wholeness
and totality of the personality.*

—Anaïs Nin

Horses do not count the passing
hours, and they have no deadlines…

PATIENCE

Victory is won not in miles but in inches.
Win a little now, hold your ground,
and later, win a little more.

—Louis L'Amour

The resting horse,
the gentle breathing, the softest nickers…

PEACEFULNESS

*Peace is when time
doesn't matter as it passes by.*

—Maria Schell

Living in the moment, forgetting yesterday and
not thinking of tomorrow, meditating in their presence…

PRESENCE

*When you live fully focused in the present,
instead of always in plans and efforts
for the future, things begin to flow
to you from that very future, it seems.*

—Elisabet Sahtouris

There is no finer mirror of
our true nature than the horse…

REFLECTION

*If you look into my eyes, you will
see yourself… Look into my eyes and you
will know if your universe is bright or
dark, infinite or finite, mortal or immortal.*

—Thich Nhat Hanh

The personal development gleaned from
horsemanship resounds throughout a lifetime…

RESONANCE

*If you have seen nothing but the
beauty of their markings and limbs,
their true beauty is hidden from you.*

—Al Mutannabbi

As in all relationships, a shared mutual respect
between horse and rider is the foundation of love…

RESPECT

*Our riding will always radiate beauty
and joyfulness when we are motivated
by respect and love for the horse.*

—Erik Herbermann

Working with horses is
closer to privilege than obligation…

RESPONSIBILITY

*A horse doesn't care how
much you know until he
knows how much you care.*

—Pat Parelli

Gather information from your senses,
from your intuition, from presence of mind and body…

SENSITIVITY

*I wonder if anyone else had an ear so tuned
and sharpened as I have, to detect the music,
not of the spheres, but of earth, subtleties
of major and minor chord that
the wind strikes upon the tree branches.*

—Kate Chopin

There are no preoccupations while riding, just
the finely tuned connection of our bodies and minds…

SERENITY

*The first thing that a rider must learn, if he
aims to become an artist, is the art of relaxation.
This means detachment, serenity, enjoyment
of work for the sake of beauty, unconcern
with success or failure, praise or criticism…*

—Udo Burger

Perhaps the only place some can let all
else fade away is in the company of a horse…

S U R R E N D E R

I have come a long way, to surrender my shadow

To the shadow of a horse.

—James Wright

Invisible, subtle signals, mental direction
and communication merge the horse and rider…

SYNERGY

*To ride well, to even stay seated, one almost
needs to become part of the horse,
and this requires an intention and focus
that seems to transcend training and commands.*

—Susan Chernak McElroy

Spending time with horses changes you; it
deepens your soul and diminishes your ego…

TRANSFORMATION

*No action is more fascinating than
the action of self-transformation.
Nothing on earth can
compare with its drama or value.*

—Vernon Howard

When horse and rider earn each other's
trust, the reward is adventure far and near…

T R U S T

*To dream anything that you want
to dream, that is the beauty of the
human mind… To trust yourself, to test
your limits, that is the courage to succeed.*

—Bernard Edmonds

Horses stretch the horizons of what we know of ourselves and our possibilities…

VISION

A dreamer—you know—it's a mind that looks over the edges of things.

—Mary O'Hara

Partnership with a horse requires a willing
sacrifice of time and a dedication to life-long training...

WILLINGNESS

*Although a riding horse often weighs
half a ton, and a big drafter a full ton,
either can be led about by a piece of string
if he has been wisely trained. This to me
is a constant source of wonder, and challenge.*

—Marguerite Henry

The mystery and wonder of
horses is like music heard in the heart…

WONDER

*The horse is an archetypal symbol
which will always find ways to stir
up deep and moving ancestral
memories in every human being.*

—Paul Mellon